EPIC
NOTEBOOKS

_____

_____

_____

STAY IN CONTACT WITH US!

✉ hello@epicnotebooks.com

⌂ www.epicnotebooks.com

(f) facebook.com/epicnotebooks

(o) instagram.com/epic.notebooks

Made in the USA
Middletown, DE
03 March 2023

26145437R00070